VOCAL SELECTIONS

WICKED
A NEW MUSICAL

D0472881

MUSIC & LYRICS BY STEPHEN SCHWARTZ

Marc Platt
Universal Pictures
The Araca Group   and   Jon B. Platt
David Stone
present

Idina Menzel

Kristin Chenoweth

WICKED

Music and Lyrics   Book
Stephen Schwartz   Winnie Holzman

Based on the novel by Gregory Maguire

Also Starring

Carole Shelley
Norbert Leo Butz

Michelle Federer   Christopher Fitzgerald   William Youmans

Ioana Alfonso Ben Cameron Cristy Candler Kristy Cates Melissa Bell Chait Marcus Choi
Kristoffer Cusick Kathy Deitch Melissa Fahn Rhett G. George Kristen Leigh Gorski Manuel Herrera
Kisha Howard LJ Jellison Sean McCourt Corinne McFadden Mark Myars Jan Neuberger
Walter Winston ONeil Andrew Palermo Andy Pellick Michael Seelbach Lorna Ventura Derrick Williams

and

Joel Grey
as the Wizard

Settings	Costumes	Lighting	Sound
Eugene Lee	**Susan Hilferty**	**Kenneth Posner**	**Tony Meola**

Projections	Wigs & Hair	Production Supervisor	Technical Supervisor
Elaine J. McCarthy	**Tom Watson**	**Steven Beckler**	**Jake Bell**

Music Arrangements	Dance Arrangements	Music Coordinator
Alex Lacamoire & Stephen Oremus	**James Lynn Abbott**	**Michael Keller**

Associate Set Designer	Special Effects	Flying Sequences	Assistant Director
Edward Pierce	**Chic Silber**	**Paul Rubin/ZFX, Inc.**	**Lisa Leguillou**

Casting	Marketing	General Management	Press	Executive Producers
Bernard Telsey Casting	**TMG - The Marketing Group**	**EGS**	**The Publicity Office**	**Marcia Goldberg & Nina Essman**

Orchestrations
William David Brohn

Music Director
Stephen Oremus

Musical Staging by
Wayne Cilento

Directed by
Joe Mantello

Original Broadway Company

www.stephenschwartz.com
Photos by Joan Marcus

ISBN 0-634-07882-8

HAL•LEONARD®
CORPORATION
7777 W. BLUEMOUND RD. P.O. BOX 13819 MILWAUKEE, WI 53213

In Australia Contact:
Hal Leonard Australia Pty. Ltd.
22 Taunton Drive   P.O. Box 5130
Cheltenham East, 3192 Victoria, Australia
Email: ausadmin@halleonard.com

Visit Hal Leonard Online at
www.halleonard.com

Idina Menzel

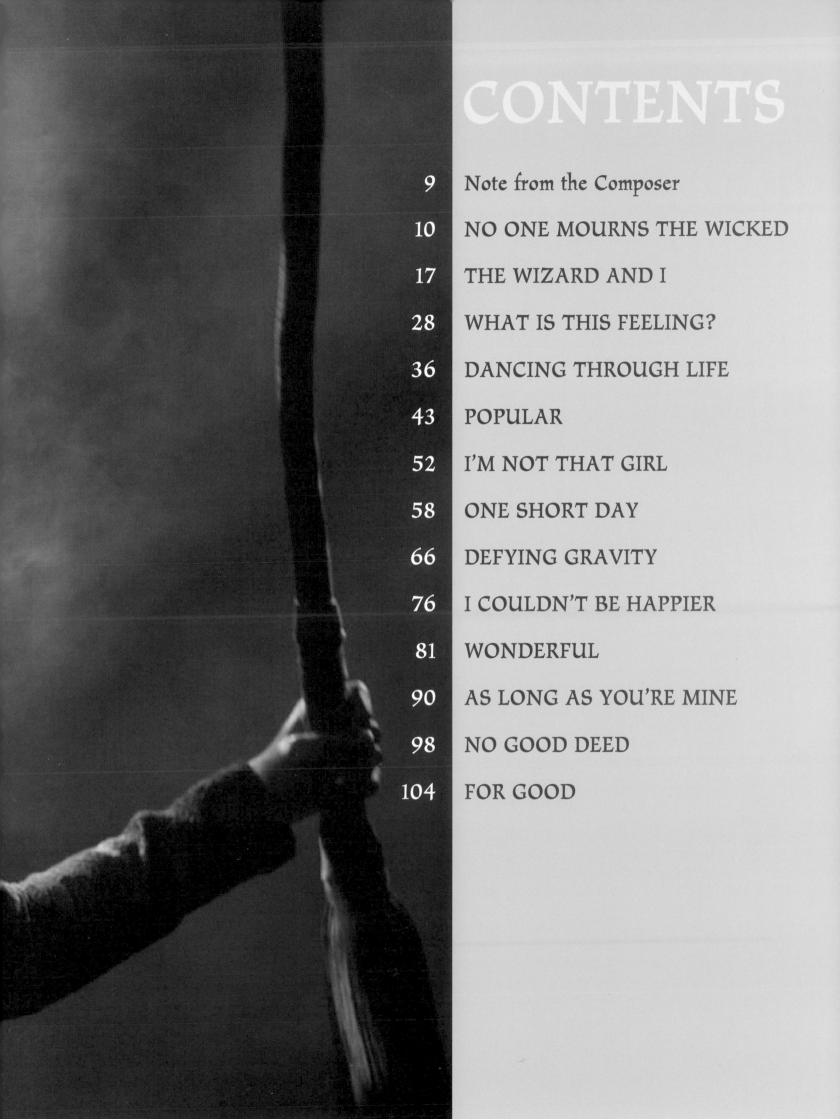

CONTENTS

Kristin Chenoweth,
Idina Menzel,
Original Broadway Company

Kristin Chenoweth

Top Left – Joel Grey
Top Right – Norbert Leo Butz
Bottom Left – Idina Menzel & Kristin Chenoweth
Bottom Right – Kristin Chenoweth

Idina Menzel

9

Note from the Composer

Several decisions always have to be made in translating the score from a show into a book of vocal selections. In the case of *Wicked*, I found it trickier than usual, because many of the songs are structured to carry the story in the show, but out-of-context would be clearer and more effective to perform in a somewhat altered format.

In the end, I chose to try to make the songs work for this medium, and thus to make changes in certain cases from the way they appear in the stage show and on the cast album. This entailed writing new lyrics in some instances ("No One Mourns the Wicked" and "Defying Gravity"), providing new endings for some of the songs ("Dancing Through Life", "Defying Gravity", "Wonderful"), and eliminating interior chorus sections, intros, or other show-oriented material from several of the selections. In addition, I excerpted one section of the opening of Act Two to create a separate song, "I Couldn't Be Happier." Two of the songs appear in the book, as in the show, as duets— "As Long as You're Mine" and "For Good" —but of course, either can be performed as a solo.

(In special circumstances, when someone needs a song in the original show format, that can be obtained by emailing me at **schwartz@stephenschwartz.com**. But it seemed to me that for most people and purposes, these changes would be preferable.)

The piano accompaniment is essentially a reduction of what is played by the show orchestra, edited so that it is playable by one person with two hands and ten fingers. It basically represents what I play on the piano to accompany the songs.

The chord symbols used should be relatively familiar to anyone accustomed to reading such symbols, but a few specific explanations are probably in order:

C5 means a C chord with no 3rd (CG)

Csus2 means a C chord with a 2nd rather than a 3rd (CDG)

C(add 9) means a C major chord plus the 2nd or 9th (CDEG)

C(add 4) means a C major chord plus the 4th (CEFG)

I want to acknowledge the help of Alex Lacamoire, Stephen Oremus and Mark Carlstein in preparing and editing this music, so that this book can be as clear, thorough, and accurate as possible.

I hope you enjoy it.

Stephen Schwartz

NO ONE MOURNS THE WICKED

Music and Lyrics by
STEPHEN SCHWARTZ

Carole Shelley

THE WIZARD AND I

Music and Lyrics by
STEPHEN SCHWARTZ

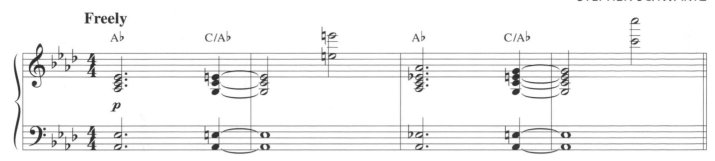

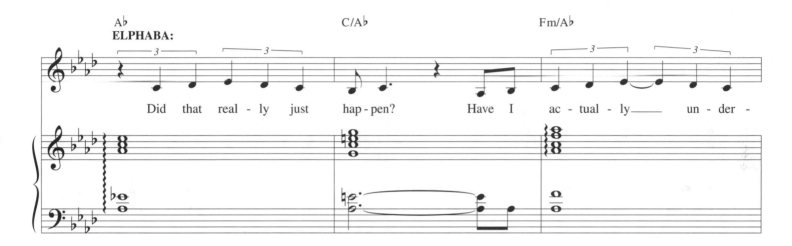

ELPHABA:
Did that real-ly just hap-pen? Have I ac-tual-ly___ un-der-

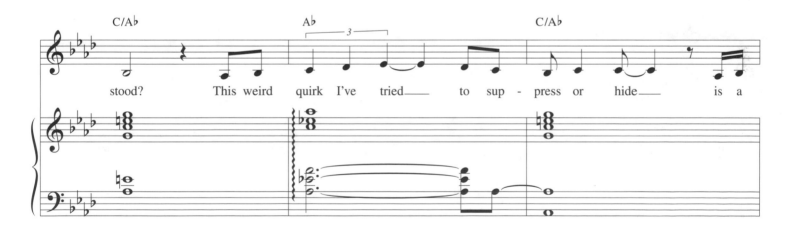

stood? This weird quirk I've tried___ to sup-press or hide___ is a

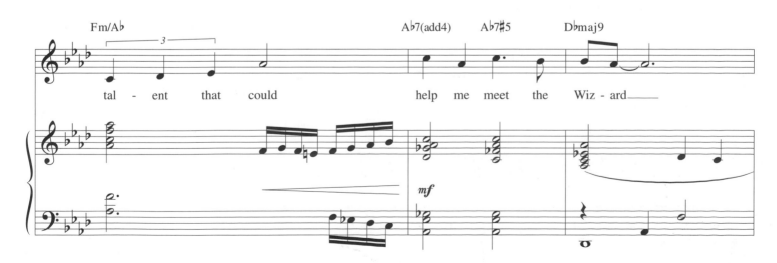

tal-ent that could help me meet the Wiz-ard___

if I make good!

So I'll—— make

Pulsing with excitement

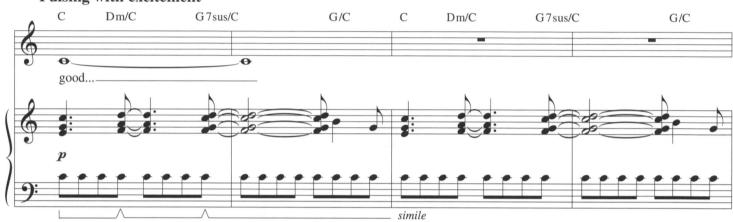

good...

simile

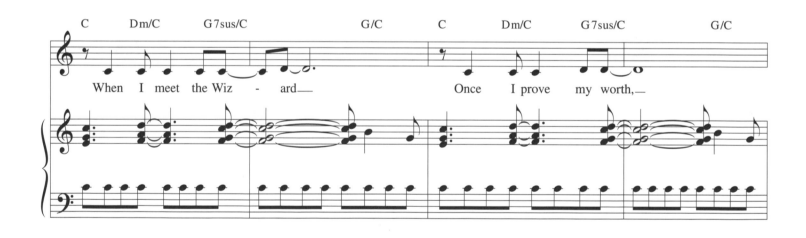

When I meet the Wiz - ard——

Once I prove my worth,——

and then I meet the Wiz - ard——

What I've wait-ed for—— since——

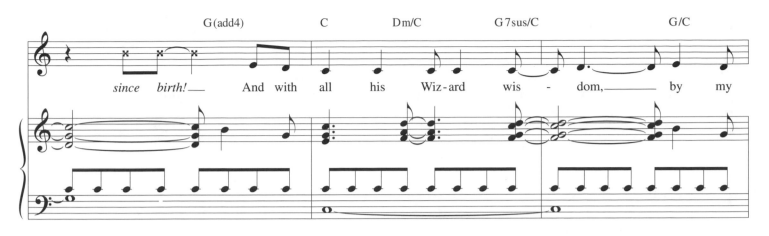

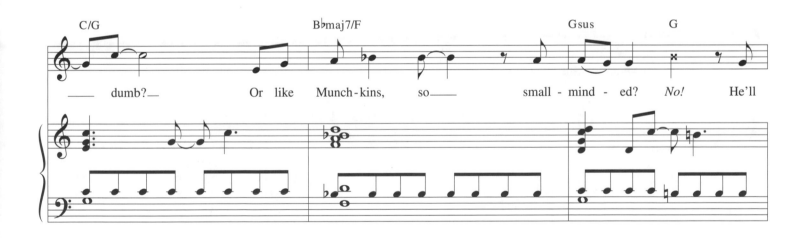

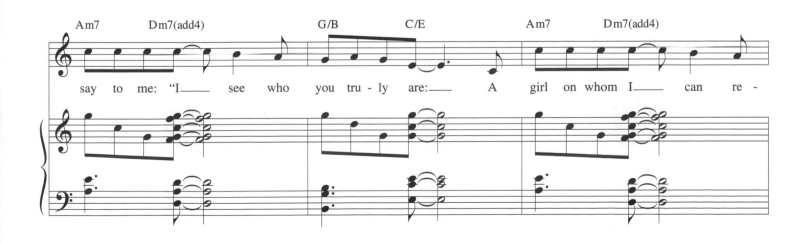

May- be at last___ I'll know why, as we work hand___ in hand,___

Più mosso

___ the Wiz- ard and I!___ And

one day, he'll say to me: "El - pha - ba, a girl who is___ so su -

pe - ri - or— Should-n't a girl___ who's so good in - side___

WHAT IS THIS FEELING?

Music and Lyrics by
STEPHEN SCHWARTZ

Allegro, jauntily pugnacious

*Carole Shelley &
Kristin Chenoweth*

DANCING THROUGH LIFE

Music and Lyrics by
STEPHEN SCHWARTZ

The trou-ble with schools is___ they al-ways try to teach the wrong les-son.___ Be-lieve me, I've been kicked out of e-nough of them___ to know.___ They want you to be-come less cal-low, less shal-low, but I say, "Why in-vite

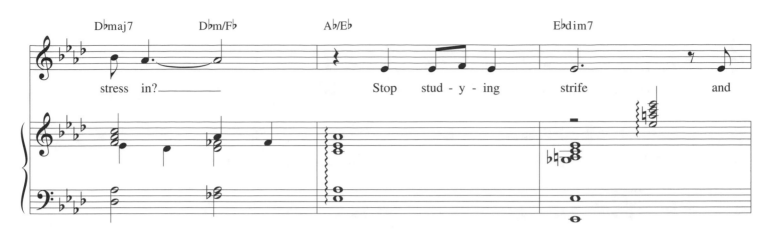

stress in?_____ Stop stud - y - ing strife and

Pop "Dance beat"

learn to live 'the un - ex - am - ined life'"..._____

mp legato

With pedal

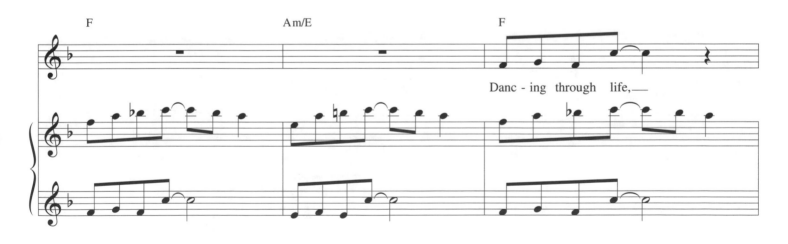

Danc - ing through life,—

skim - ming the sur - face, glid - ing where turf— is smooth._____

POPULAR

Music and Lyrics by
STEPHEN SCHWARTZ

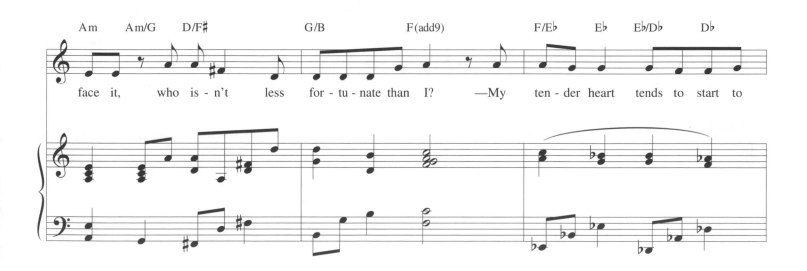

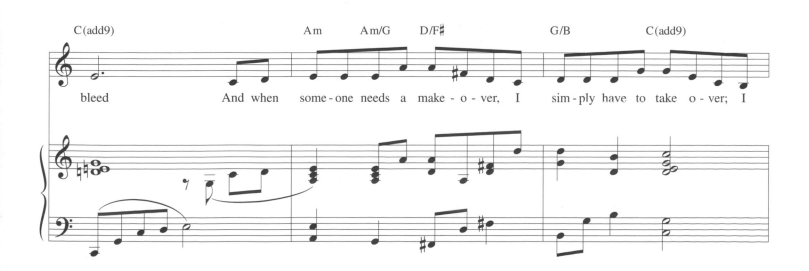

I'M NOT THAT GIRL

Music and Lyrics by
STEPHEN SCHWARTZ

Sweet and steady, like a music box

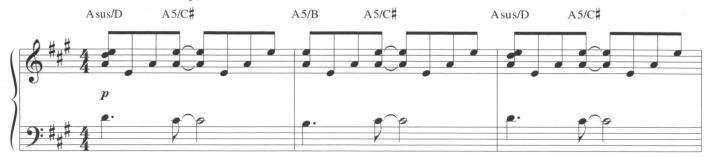

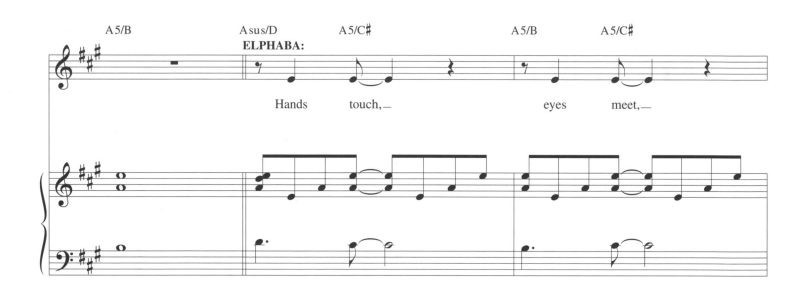

Top – Idina Menzel & Kristin Chenoweth
Bottom – Christopher Fitzgerald & Michelle Federer

ONE SHORT DAY

Music and Lyrics by
STEPHEN SCHWARTZ

Freely, sung almost in a whisper

ENSEMBLE: One short day in the Em-er-ald Cit - y...

One short day in the Em-er-ald Cit - y...

Joyfully bouncy

poco a poco cresc.

Carole Shelley & Joel Grey

DEFYING GRAVITY

Music and Lyrics by
STEPHEN SCHWARTZ

Freely, with quiet intensity

I COULDN'T BE HAPPIER

Music and Lyrics by
STEPHEN SCHWARTZ

Andante, melancholy

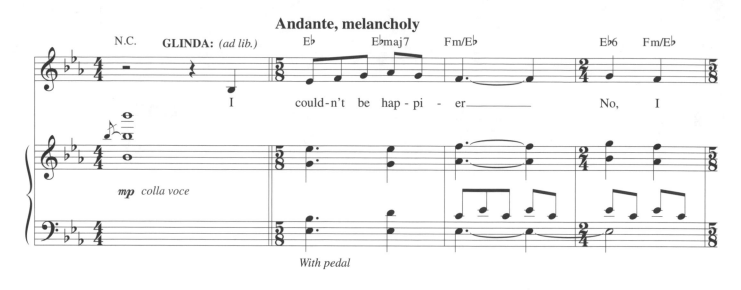

I could-n't be hap-pi-er_____ No, I

could-n't be hap-pi-er_____ Though it is, I ad-mit the

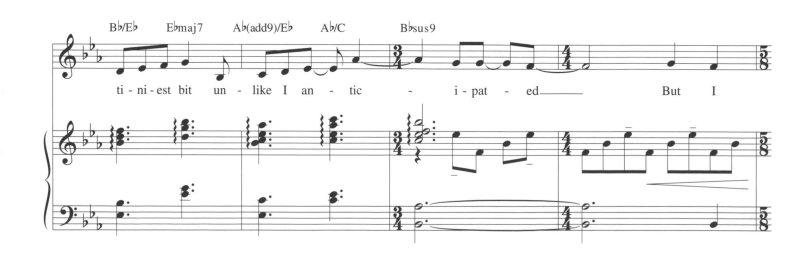

ti-ni-est bit un-like I an-tic-i-pat-ed_____ But I

WONDERFUL

Music and Lyrics by
STEPHEN SCHWARTZ

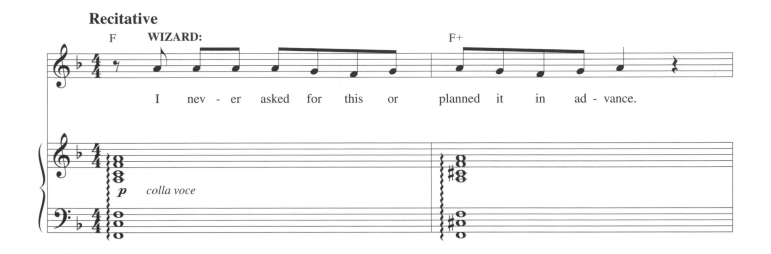

I nev-er asked for this or planned it in ad-vance.

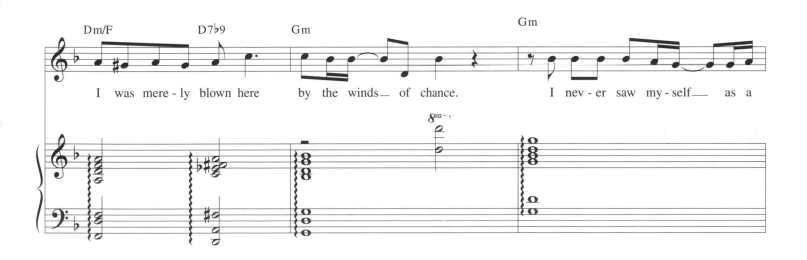

I was mere-ly blown here by the winds of chance. I nev-er saw my-self as a

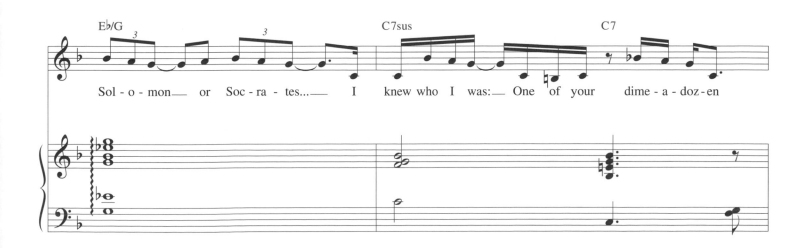

Sol-o-mon or Soc-ra-tes... I knew who I was: One of your dime-a-doz-en

In tempo, fast

AS LONG AS YOU'RE MINE

Music and Lyrics by
STEPHEN SCHWARTZ

With quiet passion

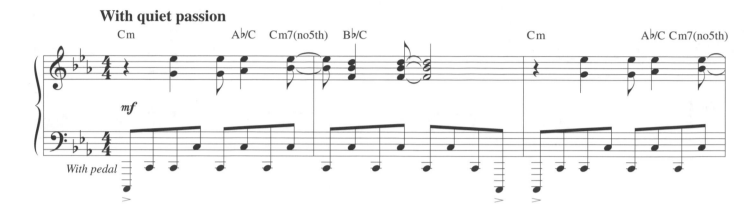

NO GOOD DEED

Music and Lyrics by
STEPHEN SCHWARTZ

Moderato, with intensity

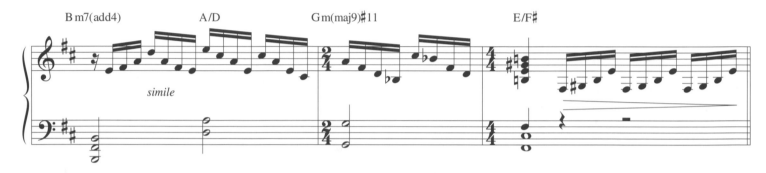

ELPHABA:

No good deed goes un-pun-ished____

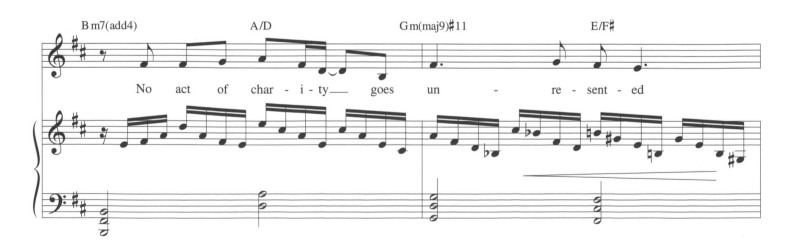

No act of char-i-ty____ goes un - re-sent-ed

FOR GOOD

Music and Lyrics by
STEPHEN SCHWARTZ

Note: When performed as a solo, sing the top melody line throughout.

Tenderly, poco rubato

I've heard it said that peo-ple come in-to our lives for a rea-son, bring-ing some-thing we must learn. And we are led to those who help us most to grow,— if we let them,—— and we help them in— re-turn.

Joel Grey & Idina Menzel